A Walk with God for Women

A Walk with God for Women

Brief meditations and prayers dealing with
experiences and feelings common among women

Leanne Ciampa Hadley

DIMENSIONS
FOR LIVING
NASHVILLE

A WALK WITH GOD FOR WOMEN

Library of Congress Control Number: 2005927199

ISBN 0-687-05392-7

Scripture quotations are from the *New Revised Standard Version of the Bible,* copyright © 1989 by the Division of Christian Education of the National Council of the Churches of Christ in the United States of America. Used by permission. All rights reserved.

05 06 07 08 09 10 11 12 13 14 — 10 9 8 7 6 5 4 3 2 1

MANUFACTURED IN THE UNITED STATES OF AMERICA

The Journey

Jesus, full of the Holy Spirit, returned from the Jordan and was led by the Spirit in the wilderness, where for forty days he was tempted by the devil. **(Luke 4:1-2a)**

It was my fortieth birthday, and I woke feeling great about it. My doorbell rang, and my mother-in-law was dropping off some cookies for me. They were my favorite, chewy oatmeal. I smelled all the goodness of a "happy birthday" baked in them. To my horror, though, my tooth broke off as I took the first bite. After canceling my birthday lunch, I spent the rest of my birthday at the dentist's!

While lying in the dentist's chair, I started thinking about what a holy number *forty* is in the Bible. Moses and the Israelites were in the wilderness for forty years. Jesus was in the wilderness for forty days. During these journeys, temptation was a constant struggle. So it was on my birthday, just when I was feeling good about turning forty, that temptation came along and made me feel, in an instant, old. I was so old my teeth were falling out!

This is the journey of our lives. Whether our journey is forty years, ten years, or eighty years, we journey with the constant companionship of temptation—but also with the companionship of a God who celebrates our lives no matter what our age.

God, remind us today, that it isn't our age that matters; it is our willingness to go on this journey with you.

Roses

"Come, let us go up to the mountain of the LORD." (Isaiah 2:3b)

I have always wanted to "go up to the mountain of the Lord," to go to a holy place where I could feel God's spirit through nature. I decided to make my own "mountain." I planted a rose garden. Each morning I go there and spend time in its beauty, praying. I love my little rose garden, and this summer the deer decided they also liked it. Each time my little rosebushes would start to bloom, the deer would eat them. They ate the blooms in June and again in July. I was frustrated. Finally my husband found a spray that repelled deer. It worked; and finally, in late August, my roses bloomed!

They were even prettier and smelled better than I could have imagined. I think the fact that I had gone all summer without them made me appreciate their beauty and magnificence even more. I actually thanked those deer for eating them earlier.

My "mountain" is my little rose garden. Yours might be time alone in prayer, spending time with a friend, or having a quiet cup of coffee. When is the last time you went to your "mountain"? Perhaps today would be a good day. If it has been a while since you went there, it might seem even sweeter today.

God, you call us daily to come to your mountain. Help us find the desire and willingness to spend time in your holiness.

Scripture

All scripture is inspired by God and is useful for teaching.
(2 Timothy 3:16)

Throughout my years as a minister I have led numerous Bible studies. I always assign certain portions of the scripture to be read between classes. Everyone goes home and reads the exact same material. When they return to class and I ask them what they have read, they all have noticed different parts of the scripture. For example, if we have read Psalm 23, one person might say, "I loved the part where the cup overflowed," and another might say, "I read that God is near me in this dark time." They read the same verses; and yet, because of their needs and where they are on their journey, different parts of the scripture speak to them. This, I believe, is God speaking to us through the Bible. Many of us are afraid to read the Bible because we fear it is too difficult or we won't understand it. But God has given it to us so that God might speak to us through it.

If it has been a while since you read your Bible, try reading a few verses today. If you read it daily, try opening your heart and mind and allow God to speak to you.

God, help us not be intimidated or overwhelmed by your holy words. May the words of the Holy Bible speak to each of us, and may we be transformed daily by them.

Distress

"I called to the LORD out of my distress, / and he answered me."
(Jonah 2:2a)

I am in distress. The pressures of being a woman are just too much. I have more to do today that I can get done. I have a million calls to return, doctor's appointments to schedule; I need to get to work on time and get all my work done because I have to leave early to pick up my son and get him to a ball game. And I know something unexpected will come along, because it always does. It isn't anything huge that overwhelms me; it is always being on this rushed schedule and never having "down time." By dinnertime tonight, I will be so tired I will not even enjoy my family. I am in distress and need to pray about this, but I feel silly complaining to God about small things. I am afraid that God has more to worry about than my schedule. And yet, these days are when I need the calming presence of God most.

God, may our time with you calm our spirits and renew our energy. Remind us that you do care about our days and schedules, and that there is no distress we can't share with you.

Holiness at Home

"But as for me and my household, we will serve the Lord."
(Joshua 24:15b)

On Sunday nights after dinner, my family lights a special holy candle, reads from the Bible, and says the Lord's Prayer. This sounds sweet, but getting my boys to come to the table is not always easy. They complain, because their favorite television show is on, they have homework to do, or they need to practice their instruments. I make them come to the table, but honestly, I wonder sometimes if doing this sacred time at home is worth the hassle.

On September 11, 2001, we were getting ready for school and work when we watched the planes rip into the World Trade Center towers. We, along with the rest of America, were in shock and felt helpless. I wasn't sure what to say to my children. How could I help them with this? My son Britton got up without saying a word and went into the kitchen. He got out our family's holy candle, placed it on the table, and lit it. I knew that the time we had spent at home in our family spirituality time really did matter to my children. I sat in the light of that candle and knew it mattered to me.

God, help us make time for you at home. We have busy schedules, so please remind us that spending time with you is the most important thing we have to do.

The Wedding

"The wedding guests cannot fast while the bridegroom is with them, can they?" **(Mark 2:19)**

My niece got married last summer. I went to her house two weeks before the wedding to help her with the last-minute wedding details. I had no idea how many last-minute details there were! We worked for two weeks, from morning until night. We tied bows, printed table cards, looked for just the right pair of shoes, filled goodies bags, and on top of it all, we didn't eat much in the hope that we could get rid of those last five pounds before the wedding pictures! I was so exhausted, and the day before the wedding I called my best friend, Brenda, and told her, "This isn't worth it!"

On the wedding day, we got up early, fixed our hair, put on our makeup and dresses (of course the five pounds were still there), and went to the church. The music started, the doors to the sanctuary opened, and I saw my niece, so radiant and happy. Joy filled me like none I had never experienced. It was worth it. It was wonderful! I cried, I laughed, I danced, and I cherished every moment. It truly was one of the happiest days of my life. The Bible often describes being with Jesus as the joy of being at a wedding. I understand that joy now.

God, you describe life with Jesus as being like a wedding. May we cherish each day with him in the same joy that weddings bring.

A New Baby

"Let the little children come to me, and do not stop them; for it is to such as these that the kingdom of heaven belongs." And he laid his hands on them. (Matthew 19:14-15)

My friend was having a baby. We all gathered for a surprise baby shower. I had decided that the best gift we could give the baby was to bless him or her, so I bought a butterfly patch for each woman at the shower and a baby blanket. One by one we said a prayer while we held a little butterfly and then placed it on the blanket. Another friend, who (unlike me) can sew, took the blanket home and sewed each little butterfly onto the blanket. We gave the blanket to the new mother to wrap her baby in as our blessings of this precious life. I couldn't help remembering how precious children were to Jesus, and how he laid his hands on those who were brought to him. I prayed that this blanket would be the touch of Christ to this new baby. Women are so blessed not only to hold our own children, if we have them, but to love, touch, and hold the babies of our friends. May our touch mirror the touch of Christ.

God, thank you that we can, in community, love your children and be for them the warmth and presence of Christ. May we reach out and touch the children who come our way today, in your name.

Letting Our Light Shine

"You are the light of the world.... Let your light shine."
(Matthew 5:14a, 16a)

I run a spirituality center for hurting children and teens. They come to me for all kinds of reasons. Some are experiencing hurt from a divorce, others the death of a family member, and some are struggling with peer pressure. I give them homemade cookies and a place to talk openly and honestly. Many days I leave my office and cry on the way home. The teens who break my heart the most are those who come to me because they think they are ugly or stupid. I look at them and think, *No, you aren't. You are perfect, beautiful, and wonderful*! Usually it is a teen girl, sitting there with her hair hanging in her face or wearing dark black makeup, trying to cover her face, which she thinks is too ugly to look at. I try my best to help her rediscover how pretty and smart she truly is. I wonder where our precious girls, and so many of us women, are getting the message that we are ugly and inadequate.

God, many of us believe that we are ugly, stupid, and unworthy. Help us see ourselves as you see us, full of wisdom and beauty. Help us be whole so that we might let our light shine.

Fighting Giants

David said, "The LORD, who saved me from the paw of the lion and from the paw of the bear, will save me from the hand of this Philistine." (1 Samuel 17:37)

My son came into the house crying, "He hit me! That big kid hit me!" He had been at the bus stop waiting for the bus, and an older boy, for no apparent reason, had punched my child! I was upset, to say the least, and immediately I went into nurse mode. I got an ice pack, had my son lie down on the couch, and held him until he calmed down. As I was holding him I thought of the story of David fighting the giant. This, I realized, would not be the last "giant" my child would have to fight. There would be many giants: drugs, peer pressure, worries about grades.

Children are not the only ones who face giants. We all do, every day. Our "giants" might be trying to juggle all the demands of being a woman, broken relationships, depression, or whatever you are struggling with today. I pray that we, like David, can face our giants with the faith that we do not fight alone, but that God is with us to help us and support us.

God, whatever giants come our way today, be near us, protect us, and give us the wisdom and strength to win the battle.

Cleaning

Wash me thoroughly from my iniquity, / and cleanse me from my sin. (Psalm 51:2)

I clean my house every Friday morning. With my two teen boys, my husband, and my ninety-pound dog, my house is a mess by Friday! At first I am overwhelmed with where to begin. I wish my house could clean itself, but it can't, so I dig in and start dusting, sweeping, and scrubbing. Before long the mess is manageable; and soon after, the house is clean and in order.

Our lives are like a house that needs cleaning. We get so cluttered and messy with the choices that we make. Before long we are totally overwhelmed with how to even begin cleaning it up. We doubt that we have the ability to fix it. Many times, our shames and fears prevent us from trying to fix it. That is why I am glad God loves us enough to cleanse us from sins. We don't have to clean this mess. All we need to do is ask for forgiveness. God will do the cleaning. I wish my house would clean itself, but I do the work. It is different when we need our hearts and souls cleaned; God does that work.

God, help us remember that when our lives are a mess, you are always willing to forgive us and cleanse us. Give us the courage and faith to come to you when we need to.

Exercise

Let us run with perseverance the race that is set before us, looking to Jesus the pioneer and perfecter of our faith. **(Hebrews 12:1b-2a)**

After watching an exercise infomercial, I ordered the video. The day it arrived I put it in the VCR and started. The process had looked so simple on the infomercial, but this woman was telling me to move and stretch in ways I hadn't ever moved! It was awful. I was in pain and sweating, and the next morning I could barely get out of bed. I was determined to get into shape, so day after day I watched the woman on the tape and followed her as closely as possible. There were days when I wanted to just give up, but I was determined. Today, a year later, I put in my tape, started stretching and moving, and it dawned on me that when I first started I couldn't even do the moves—and now I can do them almost as well as the woman on the tape.

Paul spoke of this principle as he encouraged us to run the race set before us. If we watch Jesus and practice with all our might, we can master this race. Nothing we do well happens without hard work and determination.

God, help us have the energy and wisdom to follow Christ. Give us the confidence to follow him knowing that we can win the race he sets out for us.

A Good Wife

A capable wife who can find? / She is far more precious than jewels.
(Proverbs 31:10)

My husband sent me an email today. It had information about his schedule and where he would be traveling in the next month for work. Then he included one line that made me cry. He simply said, "You are such a good wife." I cried, not because it was sweet of him to say, but because I wonder if I am a good wife. I try, but I am aware of the times I pout over nothing, I think about all the nights I have burned dinner, and I know how much laundry is sitting in the washroom right now. Still, he thinks I am a good wife. I feel so blessed. Perhaps being a good wife has nothing to do with what I do or do not accomplish in a day. Perhaps it has nothing to do with my skills as a cook. Perhaps it is simply about being loved.

I think it is the same with God. We believe we have to accomplish great and holy things to be loved by God. But what if it is much simpler than that? What if God loves us just because we *are*?

God, we try to impress you with all of our accomplishments. And yet, you love us, not because of what we do, but because of who we are. Help us love ourselves as you love us.

Missing Sleep

He will not let your foot be moved; / he who keeps you will not slumber. **(Psalm 121:3)**

Shortly before my mother died, she had to have surgery. It was minor surgery, but she was frightened of staying alone in the hospital overnight. I offered to stay with her. I thought it would be easy. I brought books to read, wore my most comfy sweat suit, and had a comfortable chair to sleep in right next to my mom's bed. However, she had more pain than had been expected. Her voice was weak, and so I soon realized that I could not sleep; I might not hear her if she needed something. Whether she needed something serious or just something like a sip of water, I didn't mind. I stayed up all night. I got very tired, but I wasn't even tempted to sleep. My mother needed me, and I wanted more than anything to be there for her.

How comforting it is to know that our God never sleeps. Day and night, God hears our smallest request and our loudest cry. And why does God stay awake with us? Because God loves us even more than a daughter can love her dying mother.

God, we can hardly fathom love as deep and as profound as your love for us. With gratitude we offer you this prayer of thanks!

Fear Not

Say to those who are of a fearful heart, / "Be strong, do not fear!"
(Isaiah 35:4)

Four houses down from me lives the kindest woman I have ever known. I don't even know her last name, but every day when I walk my dog she comes out of her house and talks to me. When my dog was a puppy and I thought he would never behave, my neighbor assured me that my puppy would be fine. When my son had his first fender-bender and I was scared, my neighbor assured me that he would be OK. When I worried that the neighbors were getting sick of my son playing his drums so much, she assured me that they were just glad he had a passion. When our nation became engaged in war, she assured me that it would not be as bad as I was anticipating. In the Bible it is angels and prophets who tell people not to be fearful. This neighbor is my angel. Whenever my heart is heavy, there she is, a smile on her face, reassuring me that it will all be fine. I doubt that she will ever know how many times she has calmed my fears and made my heart strong.

God, thank you for those people in our lives who bring us a message of strength and who lessen our fears. May we strive to be women who bring that assurance to others.

Blending Families

For everything there is a season, and a time for every matter under heaven. (Ecclesiastes 3:1)

Losing my parents was the hardest thing I've ever lived through. I kept telling myself that I was old enough not to need parents anyway, but there was a hole in my life and a longing in my heart. I wanted parents to call when my babies learned new words, and to call when I had car trouble or needed to vent.

When my husband asked me to marry him, I felt blessed by all that he brought to my life. His love, friendship, and willingness to become a dad to my two children were wonderful. One of the greatest gifts he gave me, though, was the gift of parents. Through marrying Jim, I got to have parents again—people to call when my children have accomplishments, and people with whom I can discuss my job possibilities, my hopes and dreams. The other day I helped my mother-in-law get ready for a party she was having for her friends. She kept apologizing for taking my time. She didn't realize how happy I was to have a mom I could help.

God, what blessings we are given by you. Thank you for our families, those we are born with and those we discover along the way. May each of your children find a family—a place to belong.

The Ancient Path

Thus says the LORD: / Stand at the crossroads, and look, / and ask for the ancient paths, / where the good way lies; and walk in it, / and find rest for your souls. (Jeremiah 6:16)

I love to cook. It is one of my favorite things. I don't like to cook dinner every night as much as I love to bake. I especially like to bake things that my mother and my grandmother baked. My granny's biscuits are a favorite of mine to make. My mother's fudge is another favorite. As I measure the ingredients and stir them together, I feel close to my relatives who used the same recipe and followed the same steps that I am using. I even have the plate that my mom used to pour the fudge into, and I pour our fudge into it.

God calls us to stand by ancient roads and find wisdom. As I cook, I recall the people my mother and granny were. I remember the stories they told me, how they cared for their families, and the way they loved God. During these times, they are teaching me, not only how to cook, but how to be a woman of God.

God, we often disregard the ancient paths and the ancient ways of those who have gone before. Remind us of the lessons the past has to teach us, and help us treasure and respect them.

Giving Birth

And she gave birth to her firstborn son and wrapped him in bands of cloth, and laid him in a manger, because there was no place for them in the inn. (Luke 2:7)

I always worried about poor Mary having to give birth to a baby in a stable. The smell, the straw, the unsanitary conditions have always concerned me. I felt so sorry that she had to experience birth there. I gave birth to both of my boys in a hospital, but it is odd that I remember very little about it. I have forgotten the colors of the birthing-room walls, the names of my nurses, and what my gown looked like. One thing I can remember vividly, though, is holding my babies for the first time; I remember that with great clarity. I imagine it was the same with Mary. Perhaps that stable wasn't the ideal place to give birth, but once Mary saw her son, I am sure none of those details mattered.

Giving birth—not only to babies, but also to ideas, new ministries, and our dreams—is much like that. Some of the details may seem very important and even overwhelming, but if we focus on this new person or dream we've brought into being, then everything becomes clearer, and the details that aren't so important will just fade away.

God, help us focus on things that truly matter. May the unimportant details fade away, and may the moments that are most precious linger forever.

Stepmother

"Your people shall be my people, / and your God my God."
(Ruth 1:16b)

My friend recently remarried and became a stepmother. She hopes that someday the children will like her and accept her. But right now they are angry with her and resent her new role. They say mean things to her and hurt her feelings every time they come for weekend visits. My friend was sharing this with me, and I was expressing my sympathy that the children were treating her this way. She said, "Oh, don't feel bad for me. Pray that the pain these children are feeling goes away. I have so much love to give them, and I just hate to see them hurting." At that moment I realized that she really loved these children, and for me, the words spoken by Ruth captured her feelings about them. These people, these children, had become her people, and she loved them even when they didn't love her back.

God, how easy it is to love those people in our lives who love us in return. Give us hearts that give love freely even when it isn't returned. Let us love, because you love us.

Weeds in the Wheat

"While everybody was asleep, an enemy came and sowed weeds among the wheat, and then went away." (**Matthew 13:25**)

Each night before I go to bed, I read my Bible and say my prayers. I lay all my worries, fears, and anxieties at God's feet. Usually I can fall asleep free from stress and worry, because during prayer I have been assured that God is taking care of it all. I am sure, at that moment, that God is in control, that God loves me, that God will answer my deepest prayers and do what is best for my life. I truly am at peace as I go to sleep.

However, many times while I sleep, the enemy (doubt, worry, insecurity, stress) comes, and when I awake—sometimes in the morning and sometimes in the middle of the night—I find that my peaceful field has been disturbed. What seemed so well cared for now is filled with weeds, growing uncontrollably. They seem huge, and unmanageable. The stress, fear, and anxiety not only have returned, they often seem larger than before.

God, remind us that even among weeds, you are the Gardener of our lives. Help us truly let go of all the weeds of fear, anxiety, and doubt, and grow in your light.

Adoption

When she could hide him no longer she got a papyrus basket for him.... She put the child in it. (Exodus 2:3)

I just finished dinner at my friend's home. She and her husband have two children, both adopted. I watched the parents and children interact with love and delight toward one another. I thought how lucky these four people are to have found one another. Each blesses the others in ways I am sure they never imagined.

In the story of Moses, Moses' mother was able to help with her son while the daughter of Pharaoh raised him. She was blessed to see how loved and cared for he was by his new mother. I can't help wondering about the birth mother of my friend's children. I hope she knows in some spiritual way how truly loved and blessed her children are by these parents. It wasn't easy for Moses' mother to place her baby in that reed basket, and I am sure it wasn't easy for this birth mother to place her babies in the adoption process. But what a blessing she gave to my friends, and to her children.

God, may your assurance and peace surround all the birth mothers who have faced the difficult choice of placing their child for adoption. May their children be blessed with much love and joy. For all the difficult choices we have made and that we make each day, may we feel your peace and comfort.

Abuse

When Shechem son of Hamor the Hivite, prince of the region, saw her, he seized her and lay with her by force. (Genesis 34:2)

When I first read the story of the rape of Dinah in the book of Genesis, I was shocked that a story this horrible would be in the Bible. But now, after hearing the stories of my girlfriends, I have discovered that Dinah's story is not so different from theirs. Husbands, colleagues, parents, and strangers have abused them. The saddest part of their stories is the deep shame they feel about it. Many have never told anyone their story. So instead of being shocked that this story of Dinah is in the Bible, I am glad it is there. I am glad that Dinah claims a part of a woman's life that many feel has no place in the church or in the Bible or in small groups. And I am sad for Dinah, for my friends, and for women everywhere who daily try to cope with the lasting scars of abuse.

God, please help us accept the fact that even abuse can be brought to you. Heal those who have suffered this way. Help all who have been abused to let go of the shame that surrounds abuse and to know again just how precious they are to you.

Sisters

But Martha was distracted by her many tasks; so she came to him and asked, "Lord, do you not care that my sister has left me to do all the work by myself? Tell her then to help me." (Luke 10:40)

My sister and I were very close. Her name is Paula Dean, and when I was little, I used to say that my name was "Paula Dean Me." We wore matching outfits, spent hours playing with our Barbie dolls, and went everywhere together. I will never forget the first time my sister decided to wear an outfit that didn't match mine. It broke my heart, and I realized that I was not really "Paula Dean Me," but my own person.

Martha and Mary were close sisters as well. They lived together as adults. One day Jesus was visiting them at their home, and as Martha was busy cooking, she expected Mary to help her. But Mary decided that being with Jesus was more important at that moment. Mary didn't do what her sister wanted her to do; instead, Mary did what *she* wanted to do. Martha learned a powerful lesson that day. She and Mary were different people, with different choices and different paths in life.

God, there is no relationship like that between sisters. Bless us as we travel along the path of life, not as mirror images of each other, but as women who have our own choices to make and our own journeys. Keep our hearts united with love always.

Women at the Well

Then the woman left her water jar and went back to the city. She said to the people, "Come and see a man who told me everything I have ever done." **(John 4:28-29a)**

Exactly who was the woman at the well? We don't know; we aren't told her name. We know that she was smart, because she asks Jesus great theological questions. We also know that typically she is interpreted as a sinner; we are told that she has had five husbands, not including the man she is with now. But we don't know her name.

It used to upset me that this woman lived in a time when her name was considered to be insignificant. But perhaps the absence of her name is a blessing to those of us who hear her story. Perhaps this unnamed woman is an embodiment of each of us. Like this woman, we are smart and at the same time, we are sinners. We women often feel that we need to be perfect to be with Christ. This story can remind us that Christ loves all of us, just as we are.

We are not told the name of the woman at the well. Perhaps her name is my name; perhaps it is your name. Perhaps she represents all women who deserve the attention and love of Christ, even amid our sins.

God, help us love and accept ourselves as Christ loves and accepts us.

Cords of Friendship

A threefold cord is not quickly broken. (Ecclesiastes 4:12b)

When I heard the news that my friend had been diagnosed with cancer, I felt as though I had been punched in the stomach. I decided that I would send her a card each week until she had completed all of her treatments. She called me and asked me to talk to her children, and to bless her with the holy water a friend had given her. Her other friends also helped. They cooked meals, picked up her children from school, sent cards, took her out to comedies, and did all of the other wonderful things friends do during a crisis.

About a year later I received an invitation to her home for dinner. When I arrived, the house was full of women, some of whom I knew and others whom I never had met. We ate and talked, and then my friend said, "You are here because when I was broken, you held me together. You, my girlfriends, got me through the cancer." In the midst of crisis, the cords of friendships hold us together.

God, bless our friends, near and far. Bless our cords of friendship, which are not easily broken, and which hold us together when *we* are.

Too Deep for Words

Likewise the Spirit helps us in our weakness; for we do not know how to pray as we ought, but that very Spirit intercedes with sighs too deep for words. (**Romans 8:26**)

Rarely do I have a hard time coming up with something to say to God in prayer. I have things I am grateful for, worries to share, and prayers for my friends and family. But there have been times in my life, times so deep and so profound, that I could not find the words to pray: the joy I felt when my babies were born; the sorrow I felt when my father had a massive heart attack days after my mother's funeral; when I realized God was calling me to start a spiritual-support center; when a friend trusted enough to share with me with her deepest pain. At those times, a sigh was all I could muster. But with God, who knows our every hope and dream, each thought and feeling, I suppose a sigh was all I needed to pray.

God, thank you for hearing all of our prayers—those we speak with words, those we cry out with in pain, and those that are spoken with tears and sighs. Thank you for hearing our prayers.

Dread and Fear

Do not call conspiracy all that this people calls conspiracy, and do not fear what it fears, or be in dread. But the LORD of hosts, him you shall regard as holy; let him be your fear, and let him be your dread.
(Isaiah 8:12-13)

I am an early riser. First thing in the morning, I hop on my treadmill and watch the morning news as I try to catch up on overnight events. Today, during the first five minutes of the news, there was a story about a hurricane causing loss of life, a meteor that circles the earth every four years threatening to hit the earth in the future, and an update on the war casualties and bombings in Iraq.

I have worried all day about these things. I worried about my husband, who travels to Florida often. Will he get caught in a hurricane? I worried about the meteor. Will it hit the earth when my great-grandchildren are born? Will my sons face a military draft if this war keeps up? Sometimes I think it is easier to worry about the news than to spend time worrying about my own soul. I spend so much time on worry that it leaves little time for prayer and reflection about the things God calls me to focus on.

God, help us focus on the things that you would have us focus on instead of spending all our time worrying about the things the news convinces us to worry about.

Going Alone

"Truly I tell you, this poor widow has put in more than all those who are contributing to the treasury." (**Mark 12:43b**)

My friend is a spiritual director, a mother, and an active church member. She leads grief-support groups for children and adults, and she is always on the go. She is also a widow. Looking at her, you would never know that her life has had any sorrow. She has a smile on her face and is always willing to go the extra mile. At the time her husband died, her children were infants, and the thought of raising them alone overwhelmed her. She had been very much in love with her husband and couldn't imagine life without him. His death had completely devastated her. She didn't know whether she wanted to continue living. I am so happy she decided that even in her loss, life was worth living. She has blessed so many people with her life. Like the woman in the story Jesus told, my friend, despite her loss and her sorrow, has given more to life than many. After the death of her husband she wondered if she had anything much to give, but she gave, and many were blessed because of it.

God, help us realize that we all have much to contribute to the world. Even during times of sorrow and loss, we have much to give.

Neighbors

"The second is this, 'You shall love your neighbor as yourself.'" (**Mark 12:31a**)

This scripture makes me nervous. Not because I don't love my neighbors, but because I don't see how they can possibly love my family. I have two teenage sons. They have several friends who stop by our house in their new cars with bad mufflers at all times of the day and night. Both of my sons play instruments— *loud* instruments. They play drums and bass guitar, and they work hard trying to get their band, which practices in our garage, to create music. Then there is my dog, who is huge and has a bark to match. And yet despite all of this, each day I walk my dog, and my neighbors wave and ask how we are doing. They tell me how proud they are of my boys and what good children I have. These people actually love us!

God, thank you for these neighbors who show such nonjudgmental love. May we strive to love our neighbors—even those who are difficult.

Without Words

She was deeply distressed and prayed to the LORD, and wept bitterly. **(1 Samuel 1:10)**

Being a pastor, I sit beside hurting people struggling to find a word of comfort to say to them. Many times, though, I do not speak. I just sit and listen, because as was the case with Hannah, a woman who was unable to conceive a child, their sorrow is much deeper than words can comfort. Hannah cried bitterly in deep distress. I am always humbled, then, when these people thank me for being there with them, when I have done nothing except sit beside them while they've cried.

Perhaps this is what we are called to do as women of God. Perhaps we are not expected to "fix" those who are hurting or to make their sorrow go away. Perhaps we are called just to be with them until God heals them. There are pains that words just cannot comfort: a woman who wants a baby and can't conceive; a miscarriage; a marriage that is ending; a person admitting his or her own drug addiction. We are more than words. We are women of God with the courage to be with those who are hurt, even in the darkest moments.

God, give us the wisdom to know when to be quiet and when to speak. Give us the courage to sit in the darkness, waiting for your light to shine.

Another Diet

Like many women, I am almost always on a diet. I have tried counting calories, gave up meat for a while, ate low carbs, tried the grapefruit diet, and drank diet drinks. I have tried eating what I want while increasing my exercise in order to lose weight. Still, I look into the mirror and think that my thighs are too fat and that my stomach pooches out funny. My aim is clear: to be skinny. Day after day, I fight the battle. I wonder if I will ever be finished or satisfied with the way I look.

Spiritual journeys are much like diets. Daily, I have to make love my aim and seek the spiritual gifts. I try many different ways to make it happen, to love more deeply and to seek the gifts of God. As with my diet, I need to try every day, and still I have a long way to go until I am satisfied. Maybe I will never be satisfied. Thank heavens we have people in our lives who love us even when our diets don't work. Thank heavens we have a God who loves us even when we haven't reached our spiritual goals.

God, help us love our bodies and souls as you love us.

Criticism

Wait for the LORD, and keep to his way. (Psalm 37:34a)

Sometimes I am aware, as I prepare a sermon, that I am doing most of the work. I think of an idea, develop the text, and find a cute story to introduce the concept. Other times, I am aware that God truly is writing the sermon. It flows through me effortlessly. I wish that all my sermons were inspired this way. I preached a few weeks ago as a guest pastor in the church. My sermon had been a joy to write because it was one of those times when it just flowed. I believe it was a gift from God.

After the service I was greeting people at the door. People were welcoming me and telling me how much they had enjoyed the sermon. But one person walked up to me and said, "You talked too fast, and I have no idea what your point was." I went home feeling that my sermon had been a disaster. I vowed never to preach again. Then I had this overwhelming sense of the presence of God, and God was assuring me that I would and could preach again.

God, criticism is part of all of our lives. Help us look to you, not to others, to find our self-esteem and self-worth. Help us seek to please you in all our words and actions.

Prayer Walking

"Be strong ... and keep the charge of the LORD your God, walking in his ways." (1 Kings 2:2b-3a)

My friend has arthritis in her knees. They usually are swollen, purple, and painful. She uses a walker and moves quite slowly. She doesn't walk much—mostly from her bed to her chair each morning, and back again each evening. I told my friend once that I was amazed that she still walked. She said, "I have to walk, that is when I say my prayers. It is twenty-seven steps from my bed to my chair. I have twenty-seven family members. So with each step I take, I say a prayer for one of them. By the time I get to my chair, I have prayed for each of them. I do it again each night. I pray for them, and they help me walk!"

God, may our steps remind us to pray. May we appreciate those in our lives we pray for, and may we all find joy in prayer even in times of pain.

Still Waters

He leads me beside still waters; / he restores my soul. **(Psalm 23:2b-3a)**

Whether you work in an office or at home, your day probably can be described much like mine: *go, go, go.* I have children to send off to school, work to do, meals to cook, a house to clean, laundry and ironing to do. By the end of the day I sometimes feel like mush! It always amazes me though that I can escape to my bathtub, soak for just a few minutes, and feel refreshed. Water is such a healing gift. I always wanted to live near the beach or beside a lake so that I could just stroll near the water and relax. In the meantime, I just thank God for my bathtub.

God, we can't help getting overwhelmed with the day-to-day demands of our lives. Give us the wisdom to relax when we need to, and thank you for giving us refreshment for our souls when we need it.

The Mystery of Ministry

"Go therefore and make disciples of all nations." (**Matthew 28:19**)

My friend has just started school to become an ordained minister. She has experienced a clear call from God and has started seminary, but still she wonders, *Why am I am doing this?* She is insecure, she is frightened, and even though I know how effective she will be, she is unsure of her abilities. She sat next to me at church on Sunday, and the Prayer of Dedication was printed in the bulletin. It read, "Unite your church throughout the world in continuing ministry." But my friend loudly misread the word *ministry* and said, "Unite your church throughout the world in continuing *mystery*." After church we laughed, because there was truth in her words. Ministry, and whatever compels us to do it, whether as ordained people or laypeople, is a mystery.

God, often we are insecure about serving you. Give us the faith to serve you, wherever we are called, even when we doubt ourselves.

Holding Hands

I have taken you by the hand and kept you. (Isaiah 42:6b)

As a child I loved my grandmother's hands. They were swollen from arthritis, very wrinkled, and her fingernails were never manicured. I used to tell her how pretty her hands were. Granny would laugh and say, "These are just an old lady's hands. There is nothing beautiful about these old hands." But they were! When those hands would touch me to check my temperature, or to wipe jelly or milk off of my mouth, or when she would just hold my hand, it was as if I was touched by the hand of God. I felt proud and safe and loved when she touched me. Her hands were old, and they were beautiful and holy.

God, thank you for the holy touch of precious people in our lives, and thank you for your loving touch. Bless our hands that they might be your touch of holiness for others.

Communion

While they were eating, Jesus took a loaf of bread, and after blessing it he broke it, gave it to the disciples, and said, "Take, eat; this is my body." (**Matthew 26:26**)

I love Holy Communion. I always have. There is such power for me as I walk to the front of the sanctuary, take my piece of bread, dip it into the juice, and eat. I never feel closer to Christ. Last Sunday as I walked forward, with this holy expectation I reached out to take my bread, and it would not tear loose. I pulled and pulled; nothing. I chose another part of the loaf and pulled. Finally, a tiny piece came off. This whole incident took probably fifteen seconds, but it felt like an hour, and it was long enough for the person behind me to snicker because I could not get the bread to tear. I dipped my bread and ate it, and then I returned to my pew to pray. I was disgruntled, though, because of the mishap with the bread. Then I realized that my struggle with the bread is much like my walk with Christ. It seems easy enough to reach out and take what Christ offers—peace, love, and joy—and yet I often struggle receiving it.

God, you offer us so much. Help us receive it, even when it first requires a struggle.

No Children

When Rachel saw that she bore Jacob no children, she envied her sister. (Genesis 30:1a)

I was the guest preacher at a church while the regular pastor was on a three-week vacation. The first Sunday I noticed a woman who was so delighted to be with her child. She laughed and talked to him in such a loving way. The next Sunday I saw her with three different children. Again I was impressed with her love and attentiveness toward her children. The third Sunday, she was with three more different children. They were hugging her and showing her their Sunday-school papers. The woman was delighted with each picture they had drawn. I, however, was confused, and I asked her, "Which of the children are yours?" She answered, "They all are." I said, "Wow, you must keep busy being the mother of seven children!" She replied, "I am not their mother. I couldn't have children of my own, and for years I was heartbroken. But now I thank God because I am able to teach all of these kids. I am not their mother, I am their Sunday-school teacher, and they are my children."

God, we pray for women who want to bear children and cannot. We thank you for women who mother the children of the world with love, care, and respect. We thank you for the children in our lives and for all of the opportunities you give us to love them.

Clarity

Your face, LORD, do I seek. / Do not hide your face from me.
(Psalm 27:8b-9)

Moses was given a burning bush. He was given clarity. I pray for clarity. Which job offer should I accept? How can I better manage doing your work, God, and get my household duties done as well? Am I doing what you want me to do, or are you calling me to do something else? I need clarity. I wonder why I don't get a burning bush.

I struggle with clarity. I seek it, and often, like the writer of the psalm, I wonder why God hides from me. All I know is this: It is possible for God to create perfect clarity, as God did for Moses and others in the Bible. So I will keep going, struggling and trying to figure out what God wants me to do. I will trust that if I get too far off the path, God will send a clear message to me telling me to do otherwise. I want a burning bush. I want to hear the voice of God. But for now, I trust God and myself, knowing that God gave me my brain and wisdom to use in times like these, when clarity just isn't there.

God, we are trying to walk the path you call us to be on. Help us trust our gifts of discernment, wisdom, and prayer so that we might make right choices even when we are unsure.

Thanksgiving

May mercy, peace, and love be yours in abundance. (**Jude 2**)

My mother had eight brothers and sisters, and so by the time I was seven years old, I had thirty-two cousins and seven second cousins. Thanksgiving was always held at my Aunt Dean's house, and the whole family would gather. We would have two huge turkeys, green beans, pies, and so much sweet iced tea! We would gather, pray, and then eat and eat until we were so full we'd almost be sick. We would laugh and tell family stories. These are the happiest of all my memories of childhood. These times also taught me about the way things multiply in love. We would eat for hours, and yet after we were finished, there would still be tons of food left over. I was always amazed at how much food would still be on the table. I figured that God must have multiplied it so that our fun and laughter could continue.

I don't know if God multiplied our food at Thanksgiving, but I do know that our love, mercy, and peace are always multiplied. Give a little, and God will create much!

God, you take our smallest offering and make it great. Thank you for taking our love, which often seems inadequate, and multiplying its power. We give the world love, mercy, and peace, trusting your faithfulness.

Strangers

You do faithfully whatever you do for the friends, even though they are strangers to you. (**3 John 5**)

Hours after giving birth to my son, I was trying to breast-feed him for the first time. I had read all kinds of books about it and had even taken a class. It sounded easy, but when I tried to start, it felt awkward and unnatural. I tried one side and then the other, and still I couldn't do it. I was too shy to call the nurse to help me. I started to cry.

At that moment a cleaning woman came into my room. She asked me why I was crying, and I told her. She smiled and said, "I can tell you are a good mommy. You will feed your baby. Stop crying." Just hearing that I was a good mother made all the difference, and she was right. I fed my baby. I never saw this woman again, and I don't know her name, but I pray that God will bless her for caring for a stranger who was struggling, for caring for me.

God, strangers are all around us, and often in our business we fail to even notice them. Give us the wisdom not only to notice the strangers in our midst, but also to show kindness to them in your name.

Gossip

These people draw near with their mouths / and honor me with their lips, / while their hearts are far from me. (Isaiah 29:13b)

Did you ever notice that even though our minds may be telling us not to gossip, once we start it just gets worse and worse? Then, in an effort to feel as though we haven't just gossiped, we say something like, "I will pray for her." Or when we have a confidence and it is just killing us to hold it in, we will say, "I need to tell you something so you can join me in prayer about it." There is a fine line between genuine Christian concern and gossip, and I seem to find myself there more than I care to admit.

God speaks of us acting holy with words while our hearts are far away. I think that if I truly stayed close to the heart of God, I wouldn't need to gossip. Sometimes I gossip because I am jealous; at other times it is because I am feeling superior to whomever I am talking about. Never do I gossip because I am filled with love. I want my heart and lips to match. I want to love God with my heart, my soul, and even my language.

God, help us be so filled with your love that we have no space for the things that lead us to gossip, such as insecurity, doubt, fear, or superiority. May our words be spoken with love, and love alone.

Dinner

"But now our strength is dried up, and there is nothing at all but this manna to look at." (Numbers 11:6)

The Israelites were fed manna from God for forty years as they wandered through the wilderness. They grew tired of it and complained. Grumbling about dinner has lasted through the ages. One of the most dreaded things I hear after cooking a meal is, "I hate this," or "I am not eating tonight. That smells funny." I get so tired of cooking meals that no one likes. What the people of God didn't understand is that manna was a gift of love. So are the meals I cook. It isn't what I cook that matters; it is that I made it with love. If God's people had thought about it, they would have appreciated the manna. If my children realized that their dinner is a gift of love, they wouldn't be so harsh and critical.

I wonder how many times a day God or a friend gives me a gift of love and I thoughtlessly toss it aside without appreciating it. A smile, a kind gesture, a phone call might seem like no big deal to me, but perhaps I have forgotten to look deeply enough to see its meaning.

God, thank you for the many gifts you give to us daily. May we pause long enough to see the reality of them and to truly receive them with gratitude and appreciation.

Self-Forgiveness

"Father, forgive them; for they do not know what they are doing."
(Luke 23:34b)

I was cleaning the mirror on my dresser, and when I looked into it I saw the reflection of a picture of my mother, which was sitting on the dresser behind me. There was my face, and my mother's face, next to each other. It dawned on me that my mother, at the time of this picture, and I, today, were the same age. I remember being angry with my mother in that time. I was intolerant of the mistakes she made, and I wanted her to have all of the correct answers for all my needs. But now that I am her age, I realize how young and inexperienced she must have felt. I don't have answers to many problems, and I am aware that I make mistakes daily. At that moment, when I realized that Mom was just a mother struggling to raise her children the best she could, I forgave her. I forgave her for every mistake she made and every wrong choice, even those that had hurt me. I pray that my children someday will do the same for me.

God, we all struggle to be wiser than we are, to make correct choices and not to hurt anyone, especially our family members. Please give us the same heart for forgiveness that Christ held. If he could forgive those who crucified him, surely we can forgive one another.

Confrontation

"If our God whom we serve is able to deliver us from the furnace of blazing fire..." **(Daniel 3:17a)**

I can speak in public before hundreds of people and rarely get nervous. I will try just about anything once without fear. But when it comes to having to confront someone, I go to pieces. Like many women, I want to be liked by everyone, and confrontation nearly assures me that someone won't like me anymore. I can't sleep, I feel sick, and I get heartburn. I will do anything to avoid confrontation. But when it has to be done, I call on this scripture and remember Shadrach, Meshach, and Abednego, who faced a fiery furnace of their own. They spoke boldly, declaring that God would take care of them. I wonder, though, if even in their faith and bravery they were frightened and dreaded the furnace. Before I go to the furnace of confrontation (or some other similar situation), I recall this story and ask God to care for me in the same way. I don't know whether those three men were frightened, but I am. And yet, knowing that God will go with me gives me the strength I need.

God, whatever fiery furnace we are called to enter—confrontation, sickness, struggling with our finances, worries about our families—remind us that you are with us. Protect us with your love, and give us strength.

The Mountains

I lift up my eyes to the hills— / from where will my help come?
(Psalm 121:1)

I grew up in Kentucky and Southern Ohio. I had never seen a mountain. I thought they were tall, straight on both sides, and always purple, as in "purple mountain majesties." When I moved to Colorado, I discovered that the mountains change throughout the seasons and even throughout the day. At times they are green and lush. In the fall, as the aspen trees change to gold, the mountains sparkle and shine. In the winter they are purple, with snow on the caps. During the day, they can be covered with white wispy clouds and look mysterious, or seem angry as dark storm clouds cover them. They change, and each time I look at them I realize how truly majestic and beautiful they are. And the more I look at them, the more I love them.

It is the same with God. Many of us carried images of God from childhood, and, as we matured, our images changed and deepened. But still, God is majestic. The more we pray and truly think about God, the more beautiful God becomes.

God, give us the wisdom to be still and to focus on your beauty and majesty each day. May our understanding of you and your goodness deepen as we reflect upon your glory.

Searching the Heart

I the LORD test the mind / and search the heart. (**Jeremiah 17:10**)

I try so hard to do the right things, to say kind words and to be a loving presence in the world. I really do, but the day-to-day demands and my hectic schedule can cause me to lose focus in no time at all. Before I know it, I am so caught up in whatever is happening that my loving presence has evaporated and my words are far from kind. I wake up determined to be God's presence in the world, and, more nights than I care to admit, I go to bed feeling as though I have failed! I love this passage from Jeremiah, because in it God tells us that God will search our hearts and minds and know the truth. I truly have the desire to be the person God calls me to be. I pray that God will look beyond my actions when I fail, and into my heart, and see the true me. I pray that God will see the desires of my heart and forgive me when I fail to be the person I hope to become.

God, look deeply into our hearts and see the women we truly are striving to be. We desire to be your presence in the world. Please be patient while we struggle to grow into the women you call us to be and that you know we already are in our hearts.

Doorposts

And write them on the doorposts of your house and on your gates.
(Deuteronomy 6:9)

The words of this scripture passage follow the great commandment to love the Lord our God with our hearts, minds, and souls. We are then told to write these words on the doorposts of our houses. I always wondered why. What good would that do? Then a friend of mine gave me a little wooden cross with a short ribbon tied on it. I wasn't sure where to put it, so I hung it on my front doorknob until I could find a better place for it. Each day as I opened the door, I touched that cross and was reminded that I am a Christian, that I am deeply loved by God, and that I need to show the same love to others throughout the day. I have never moved that cross to a "better" location; it is where it should be. For each time I walk through my door, I am reminded to love God and to love others. I understand why God told us to hang a reminder on our doorposts.

God, remind us daily to honor you with our love and concern for others. Whether we are at home, work, church, shopping, or driving, we are called to love.

Giving Thanks

Rejoice always, pray without ceasing, give thanks in all circumstances.
(1 Thessalonians 5:16-18a)

I woke up today with so many things to do—grocery shopping, work, writing... My list is usually long, but today's is especially long. I turned on the television, and the weather report said it was going to be cold and rainy all day. I was disappointed. I needed a sunny, warm day, not a cold, sleepy day, to get all of my tasks done! Then I thought of this passage in 1 Thessalonians and decided to say a prayer of thanks to God for the cold day.

As I gave thanks, the cold grayness settled around me. Instead of fighting it and struggling to feel energized, I realized how hard I have been pushing myself lately. I felt the gray day calling to me to slow down, to stop pushing, and to try and take it easy. Throughout the day, instead of going a hundred miles an hour, I am going at a pace that is good for me and good for my soul. Instead of being disappointed, I am going to give thanks. God has many lessons to teach me, even in my disappointments.

God, before we start to rail against our disappointments, gently remind us to give thanks and to learn from them. May all you give to us be received with thanksgiving, for you are in all things and in each moment.

Sing!

Sing aloud to God our strength; / shout for joy to the God of Jacob.
Raise a song, sound the tambourine, / the sweet lyre with the harp.
(Psalm 81:1-2)

I took piano lessons when I was six years old. I quit them before my seventh birthday, and that was the end of my hopes of ever becoming a good musician. I regret that choice. However, my uncle, who lives in Kentucky, makes dulcimers. I have one, and I get it out and strum away singing all my favorite hymns. I love singing to God. No matter what my mood, I start singing and I feel better. However, my children can't stand it. They are good musicians, and they tell me how my dulcimer is out of tune, how my chords do not match the notes I am singing, and that I am not singing in tune. It has become a huge family joke, but I don't care. I am not singing to sound good. I am singing in praise of God. So I sing and sing, out of tune, but loud and full of spirit. Join me today and sing a song to God!

God, even when we aren't using our mouths to sing, may you hear the singing of our hearts and souls. We love you and praise you with joy!

Gifts and Prayers

Then, opening their treasure chests, they offered him gifts of gold, frankincense, and myrrh. **(Matthew 2:11b)**

Advent is such a busy season, and I try to make it more manageable by buying Christmas gifts all year long. No matter what the month, I am looking for just the right gift for each member of my family and friends. I shop at the mall, look through catalogs, and search the Web. I want something that will be perfect for each one of them.

The other day as I was looking through a catalog, I had an epiphany: I spend more time looking for Christmas gifts for these people than I do praying for them. The wise men brought gifts to Christ, but before they offered them, they knelt down. Do you think they prayed in that moment, thanking God for this child? I am going to try to do the same. I need to get the shopping done, but I also need to pray for the people I am shopping for. Each time I find the perfect gift or a gift possibility, I am going to pause and pray for the person.

God, please remind us that while our gifts are precious to those whom we love, our prayers are the best gift we can ever give them. May we pause and pray for those we love, knowing that you hear our prayers.

Running the Show

Lead me to the rock / that is higher than I; / for you are my refuge.
(Psalm 61:2b)

I am something of a control freak. I like to have things done well and on time. My house is usually orderly if not clean, dinner is cooked, the work is done, and I usually am on time in transporting my children to and from their activities. I have things under control. But then there are the days when I hit a wall and I feel resentful of all the things I am in charge of. These are days when I don't want to cook dinner or clean the house, and I don't want to run the kids here and there. I do it, but I am resentful. I realize that much of what I do, I do because I don't believe anyone else can do it. And I am afraid that if I let things go, I will no longer be of value to my family. I control myself into a space of resentment and anger.

God, remind us that we are not called to control the world. You are the one who controls the world. Remind us that we can let go of control and still be loved and accepted. You are a rock that is higher than us!

Help from God

Though we stumble, we shall not fall headlong, / for the Lord holds us by the hand. (Psalm 37:24)

I went to a women's retreat. I was expecting to listen to lectures, do some Bible studies, and chat with the other women there. Much to my horror, I learned that we would be learning about trust, and we were led outside to a "ropes course." One of the steps on the course was an activity where we had to walk across a board that was six feet high in the air, and we had to trust the other women to hold our hands so that we would not fall. I didn't want to do it. I tried to get out of doing the activity, but I did it, and of course, I started to fall. To my joy, the other women steadied me, just as they had promised to do. To my amazement I actually ended up having a great time during the activity.

God promises to hold us by the hand and to catch us when we stumble or fall. Why is it so difficult for us to trust God, and to trust other women?

God, we know you are there to catch us when we fall. We know that our friends are willing to help us as well. We pray that you replace our fear with gratitude and trust that we will not fall but will be held by your hand and the hands of those who love us.

Getting Older

You shall be a crown of beauty in the hand of the LORD. (Isaiah 62:3a)

I got up this morning, started to brush my teeth, and noticed just how old I look now. I have wrinkles and age spots, and my skin isn't as firm and smooth as it used to be. I looked in my makeup basket at all the products I have bought in the past year, trying to look better—anti-aging creams; cover-up stick; hair thickener; separate moisturizing lotions for every part of my body; and cosmetics promising to make my lashes longer and my cheeks brighter. While I realize that this is ridiculous and I want to love myself as I am, I would be lying if I said I didn't care. Obviously I care enough to have a whole store's worth of merchandise in my own bathroom. But underneath it all, I am aware that God loves me and thinks that I am beautiful. God couldn't care less about my wrinkles; God loves my heart and soul. I am beautiful—wrinkles, age spots, sagging, and all; I am beautiful, and so are you!

God, how can we even begin to thank you for loving us with such depth? Remind us of our beauty—not only our physical beauty but also the beauty of our hearts, souls, and actions.

Caring for Christ

"For I was hungry and you gave me food, I was thirsty and you gave me something to drink, I was a stranger and you welcomed me, I was naked and you gave me clothing, I was sick and you took care of me, I was in prison and you visited me." (Matthew 25:35-36)

We had a new neighbor move in, and I baked muffins, took them to her, and welcomed her to the neighborhood. My friend's husband has been laid off from work for a long time, and so I bought this friend lunch yesterday. I cleaned closets last week and took bagfuls to Goodwill, and today I filled a bag with canned goods to take to church on Sunday. I sent a card to another neighbor, who is in the hospital, and another card to a friend who is in a rehabilitation facility trying to put his life back together. These are the sorts of things we do as women on a daily basis, and never think twice about. They are just cards we send, meals we buy, and closets we clean. But in the midst of these activities, we are doing the very things Christ calls us to do: to care for those who are sick, disadvantaged, and outcast.

God, help us celebrate that even in the simplest daily tasks of being women, we often bring you joy and honor.

Love

"Therefore, I tell you, her sins, which were many, have been forgiven; hence she has shown great love." (Luke 7:47)

In this story in Luke 7, a woman anoints the feet of Jesus with her tears and kisses, and she is criticized for it. The disciples are angry because a sinner is being so intimate with Jesus. And yet, Jesus stands up for her, saying that she will be remembered not for her sins, but for her love.

At the end of the day, I often criticize myself for all of the things I have done wrong. I think of the unkind thoughts I have had, the times I lost my temper or spoke out when I should have stayed quiet. I am painfully aware of each mistake I made. I am much like the disciples, being critical of the sins and not noticing the acts of love I have also done during the day.

I like this story, because it reminds me that Christ does not look at us as we look at ourselves. Christ forgives our sins and remembers the loving acts we have done.

God, help us see ourselves as Christ sees us. Help us forgive ourselves of our sins and remember the love we have expressed. Remind us, when we start to judge another person, to look at that person through Christ's eyes as well. For we know that our sins and the sins of others are forgiven, but love remains forever.

E-mail

Although I have much to write to you, I would rather not use paper and ink; instead I hope to come to you and talk with you face to face, so that our joy may be complete. (2 John 12)

I love e-mail. E-mail makes it so easy to write and keep up with those I love. My niece lives in Kentucky; my brother, sister, and many friends live in Ohio; and I have dear friends in Florida and California. We usually e-mail weekly, and sometimes even daily. In the past I usually waited to write a letter until I had big news. But with e-mail, I tell my family and friends even the smallest details of my day. Cell phones are great as well, because they make it easier for people to locate one another. It used to be that my loved ones had to be at home before I could reach them and talk to them. Now, I can be at a ball game, and they can be at the store or at work, and we can connect. Yet still we are apart, and how I long to see them face-to-face to laugh and be together. Writing e-mails and calling on the phone are wonderful, but nothing replaces being together and sharing a hug.

God, please be near the people we love and desire to be with today. Hold them, hug them, and watch over them. May we all be safe and healthy while we are apart, and may we find ways to connect until we can meet face to face.

Cups Overflowing

You prepare a table before me / in the presence of my enemies; you anoint my head with oil; / my cup overflows. **(Psalm 23:5)**

I was making gravy the other night for dinner. I had cooked a pot roast and was dipping a measuring cup into broth and transferring it into a skillet in which to make the gravy. I would dip the cup and it would be full, but by the time I got the cup to the skillet it would only be about a quarter of a cup full. I looked at the bottom of the cup and noticed that it had a small crack in it. The broth was pouring out of the bottom of the cup. I thought about the twenty-third psalm, and the cup overflowing. I also thought about my life. Do I have cracks in my spiritual cup that keep it from overflowing? Are fatigue, overcommitting, and demanding perfection both of others and myself creating cracks in my cup? Are there places in my life that are not whole, places where my joy is draining out of instead of overflowing? God wants our cups to overflow with goodness, joy, and love. If they are not, perhaps we need to look closely and notice where the cracks are.

God, you know the places where our spirits are weary and wounded. Heal us, we pray, so that we might be filled and overflow with goodness, mercy, and love.

Turning to Salt

But Lot's wife, behind him, looked back, and she became a pillar of salt. (Genesis 19:26)

When I look back at my life, I feel complete, happy, and satisfied. Even the mistakes I have made don't seem so huge anymore. While it hasn't been perfect by any means, it has been my life, and I am pleased with it. My children are teenagers now, and I realize that my life is about to change. I have been reviewing the past, looking through their picture albums and baby books. I also have been trying to imagine what my life will be like when they are off to college. On the one hand, I am excited when I think of all the time I will have, and not having to worry about their day-to-day schedules. On the other hand, I am sad that they have grown, and I worry about what I will do with myself when they are not home. This story of Lot's wife reminds me that we are called to look forward with anticipation and not to look back in fear. So I am looking forward.

God, help us look forward, even when the past is attractive and beautiful compared to the unknown future. Help us look to the future with hope, and not to fear it.

Waiting

"Beware, keep alert; for you do not know when the time will come."
(Mark 13:33)

My favorite time of day is when everyone is home, the business is settled, and we are relaxed. It is a rare and precious moment. Whenever another family member is away from home, I am "on watch." You wouldn't know it by looking at me. I am doing dishes, checking e-mail, watching television, reading; but at the same time, I am watching and waiting for whoever isn't home to get here. I hear every car pass the house, I listen for their voices, and I regularly check the time to see if they are later than I think they should be.

I think this is what Jesus called us to do when he told us to watch for his return. We still can participate in daily life. We can work, play, go to the movies; but we are called to be aware that he could be here at any moment. I think that waiting for Jesus means more than anticipating the end of time. I think it means to wait for him at each moment. While we are doing our everyday tasks, we listen for his voice and anticipate his presence.

God, please give us the wisdom to wait for Christ as we wait for our loved ones. May we be attentive to his presence and voice, even in the midst of our daily routines.

Laughing

The LORD said to Abraham, "Why did Sarah laugh, and say, 'Shall I indeed bear a child, now that I am old?' Is anything too wonderful for the LORD?" (Genesis 18:13-14a)

I am a laugher. I not only laugh at jokes and cute things kids say and do, but I am also one of those people who laugh at awkward times. As a child, I would laugh when I got into trouble, and when something funny happened in the quiet sanctuary. I still laugh in the middle of arguments and at the wrong times! I figured out that I laugh when I am nervous. As the tension builds, so does my desire to laugh. I have gotten into trouble more than once for this!

In the story in Genesis 18, I think that Sarah laughed not because she was in trouble or because she was nervous. I think she laughed at the glory of God. God is so wonderful that sometimes our joy can't be expressed with words. It is expressed with laughter. For all of us women, I pray that the glory of God shine so brightly today and tomorrow and the next day that our laughter, like Sarah's, will fill the world. There is enough sorrow, there is enough pain, and there is plenty of serious reflection. May our laughter be a gift to God and to the world.

God, you are so marvelous that our laughter is a prayer. Thank you for the miracles that come our way, for your creativity and never-ending love.